Under the Sea

By

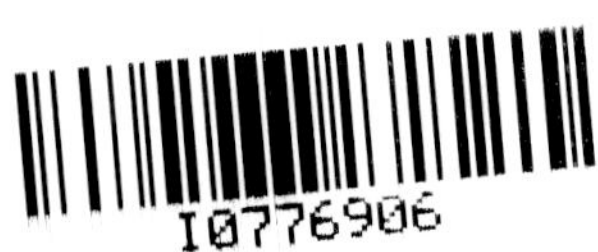

Lillian Pasten

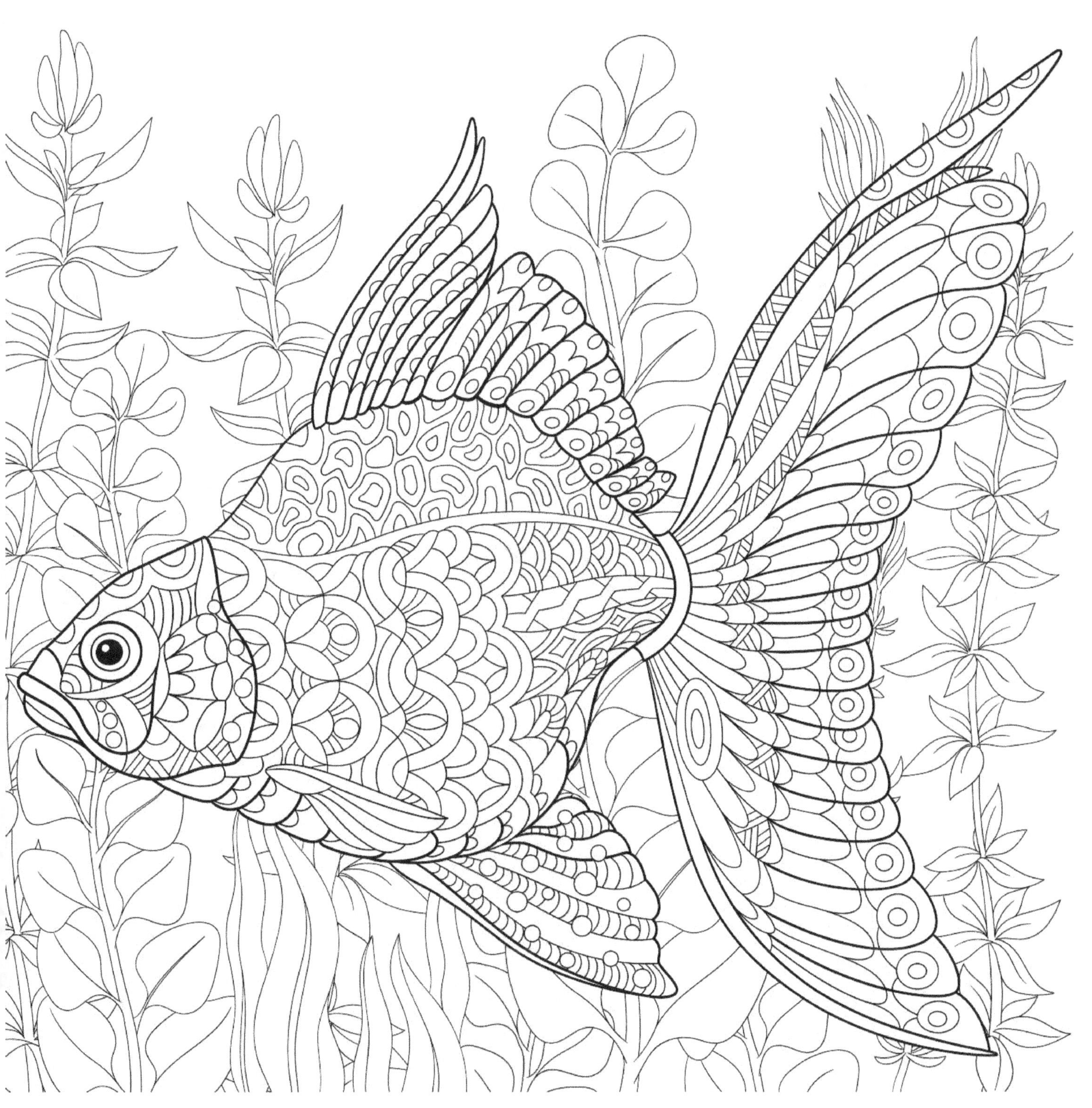

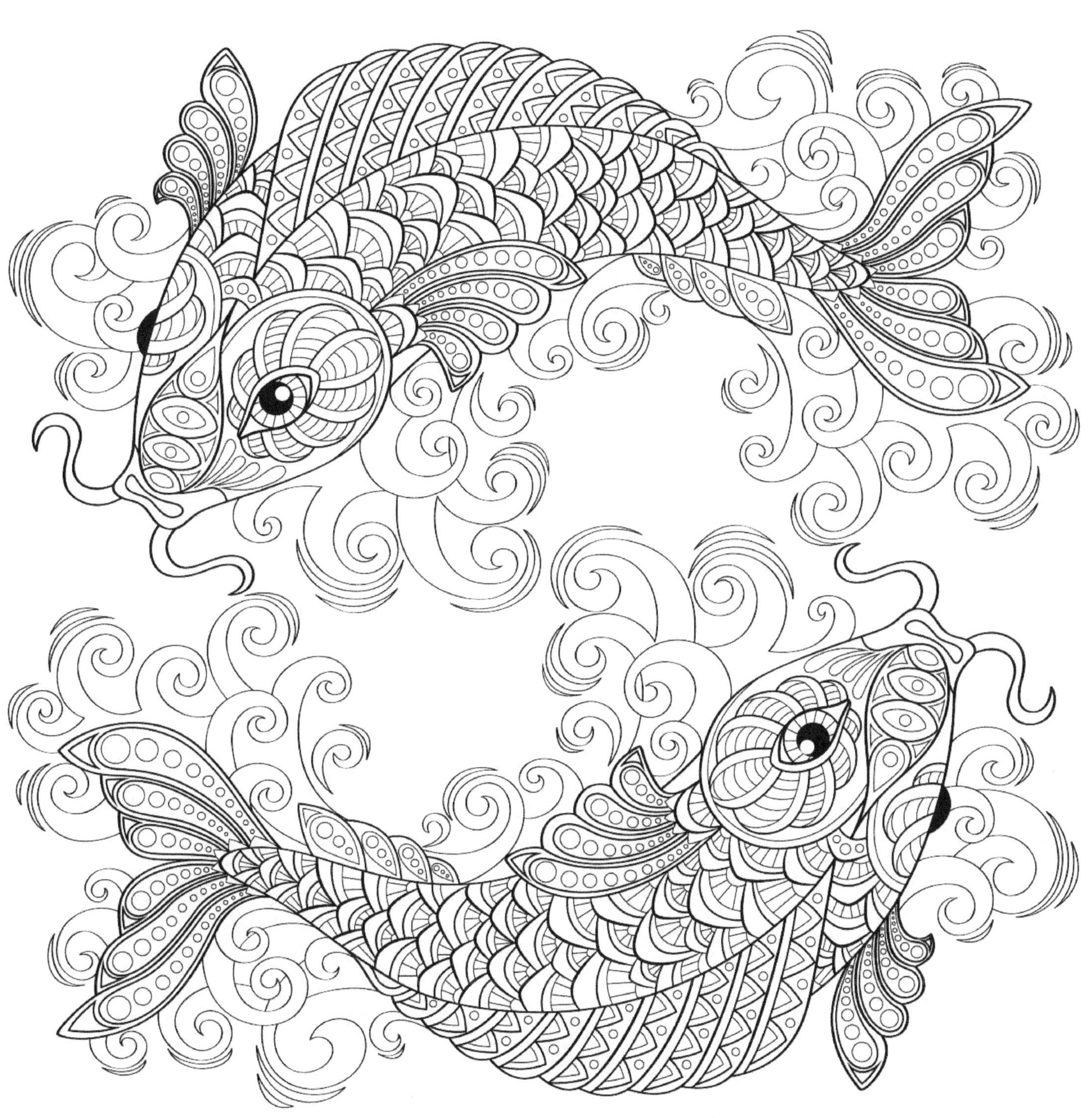

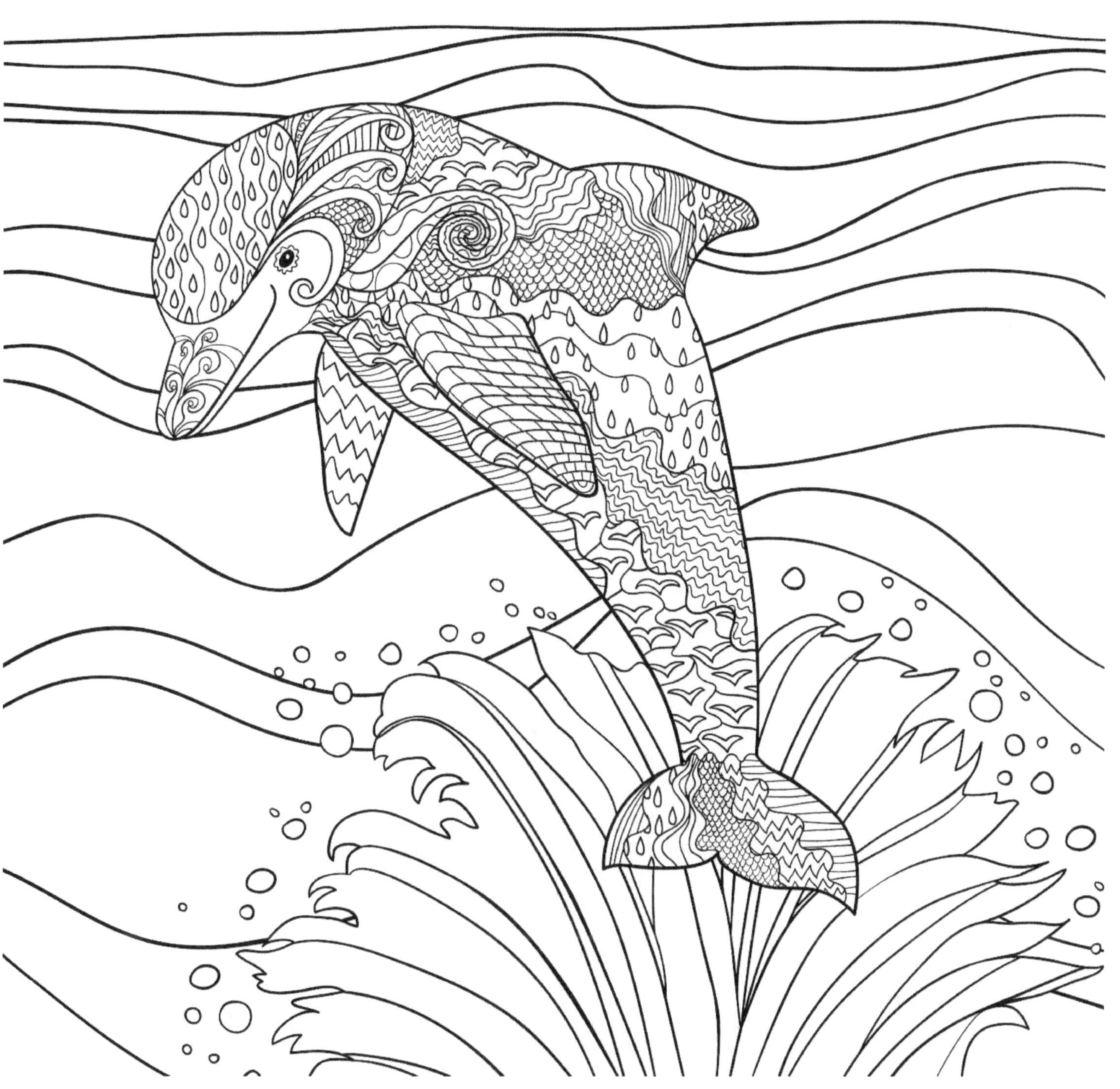

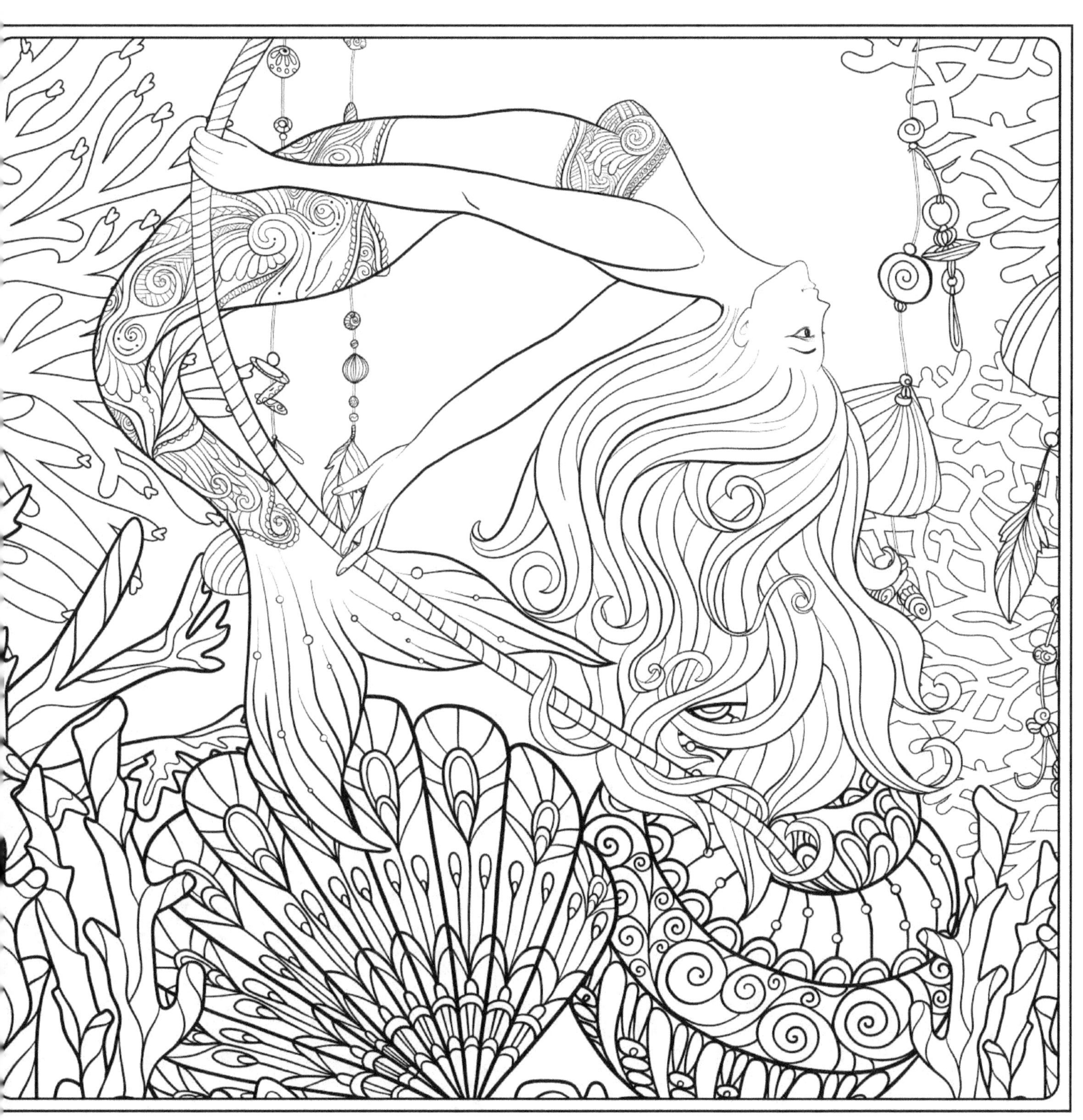

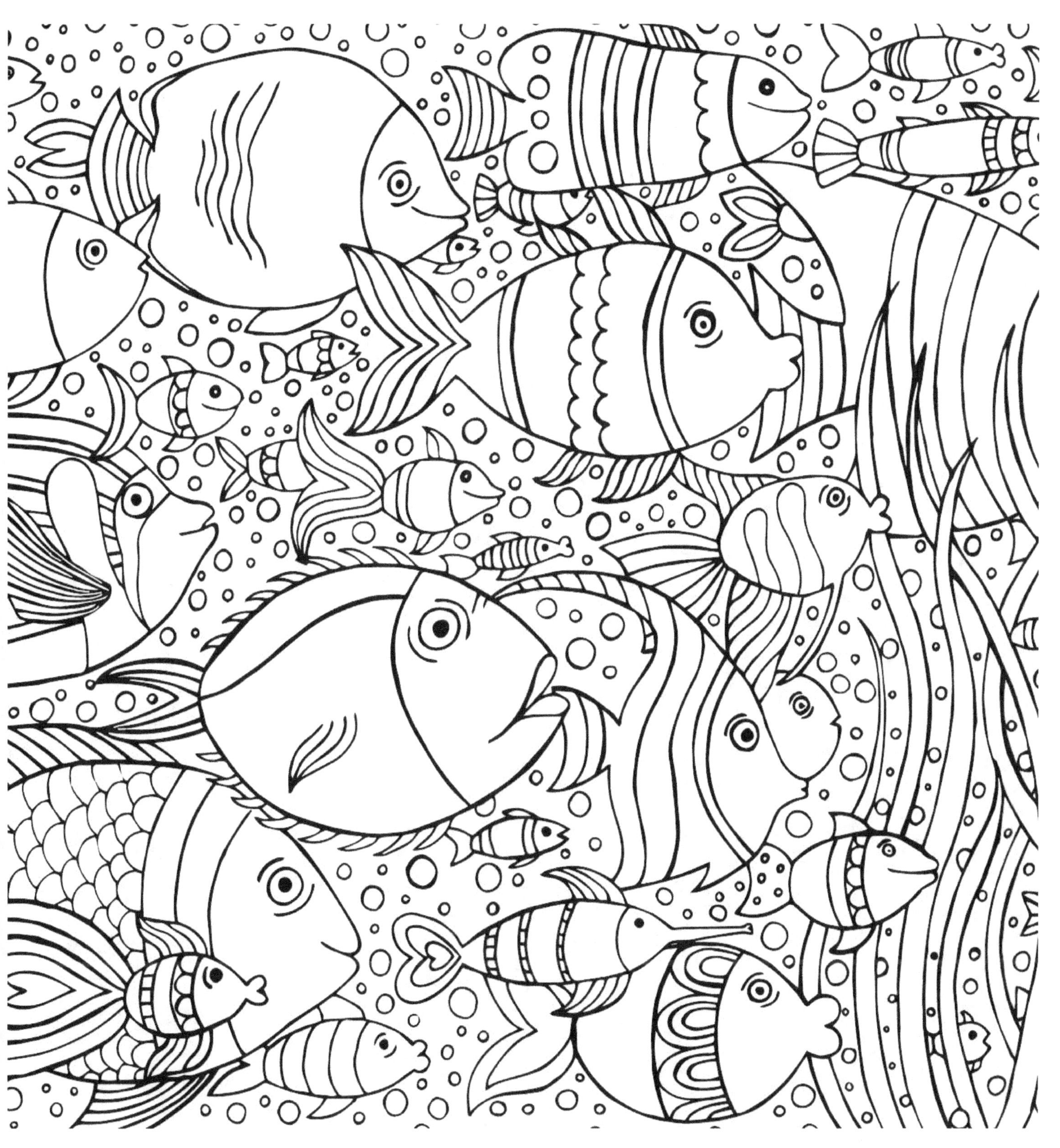

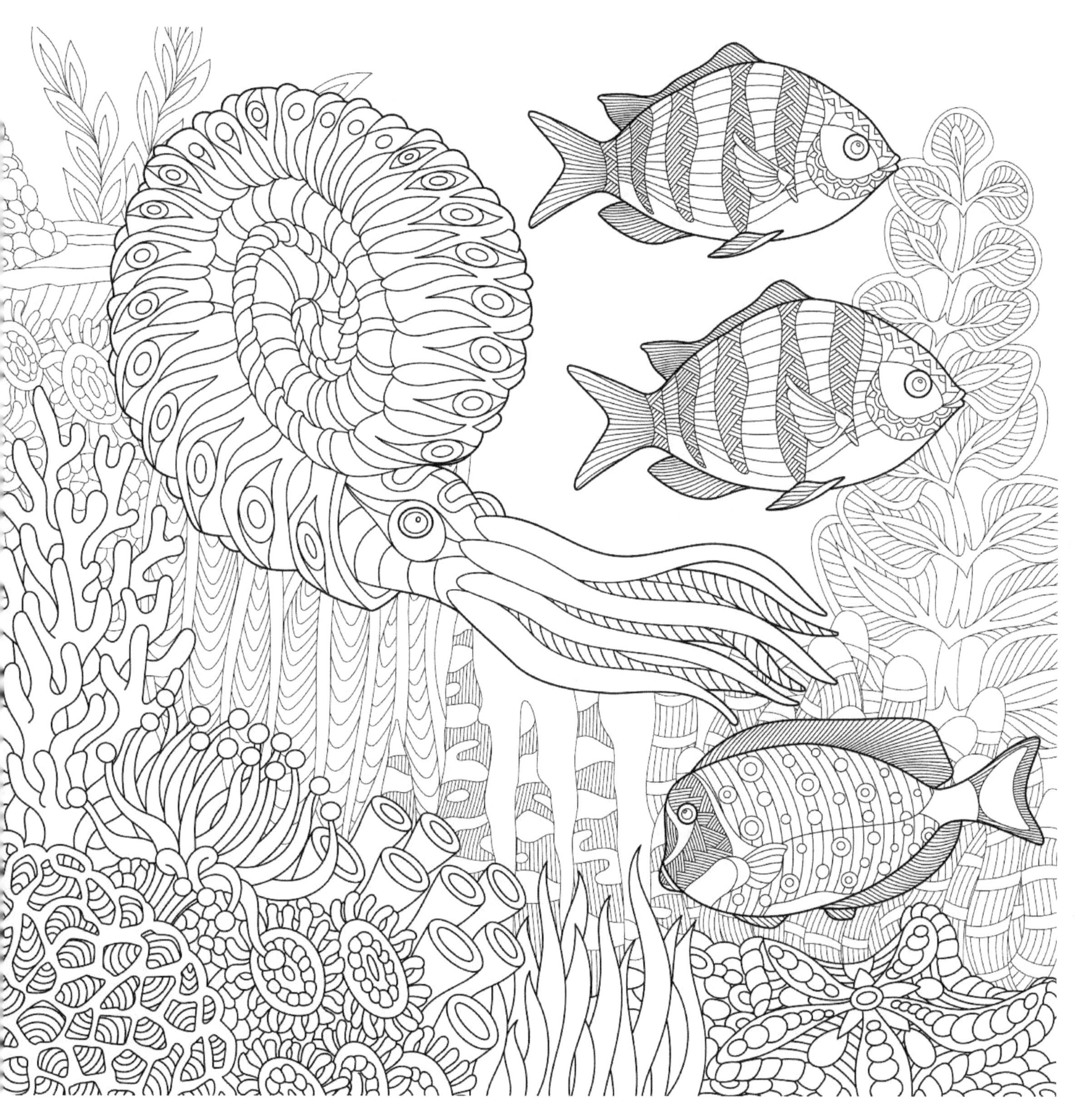

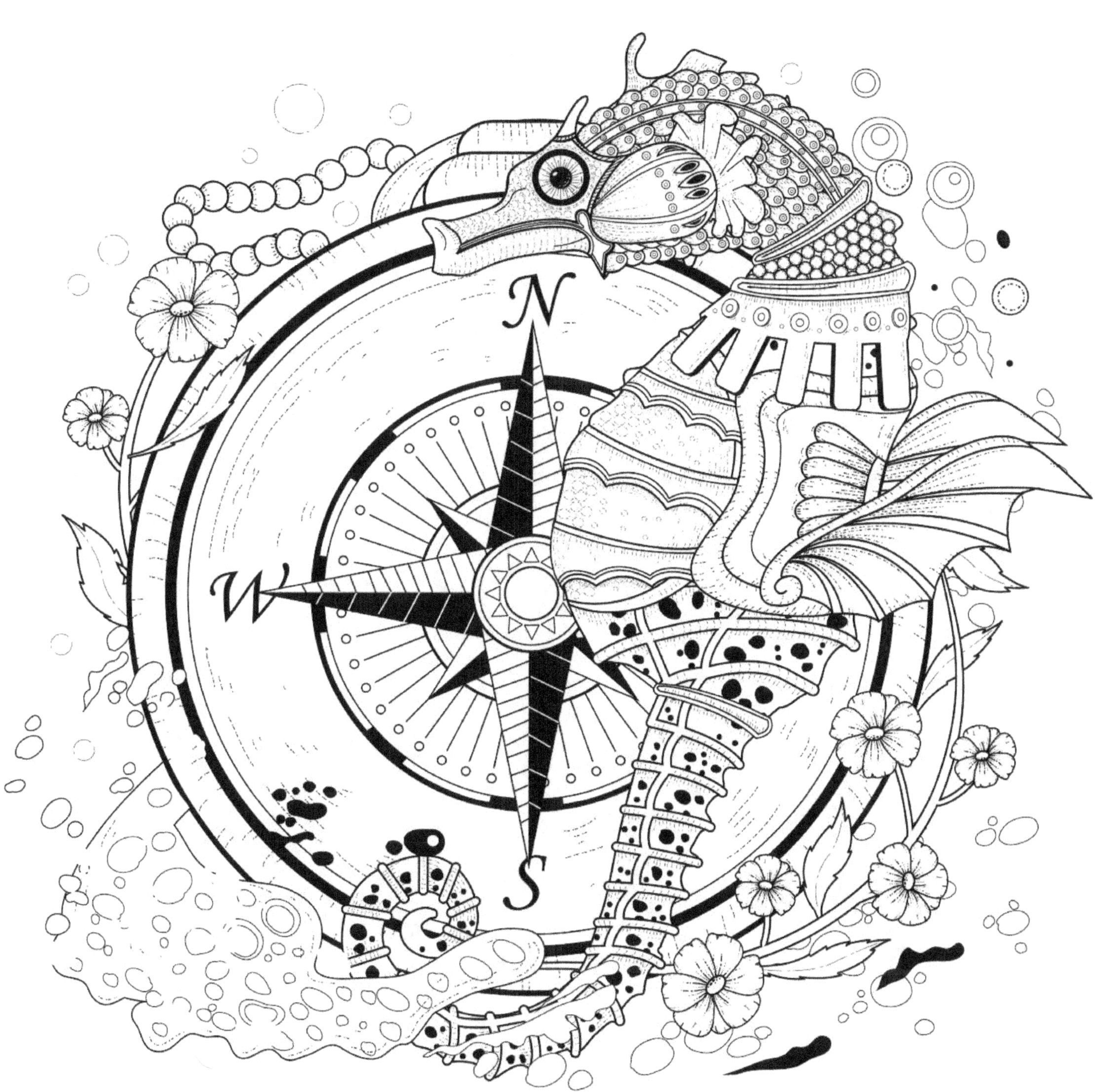
N
W
S

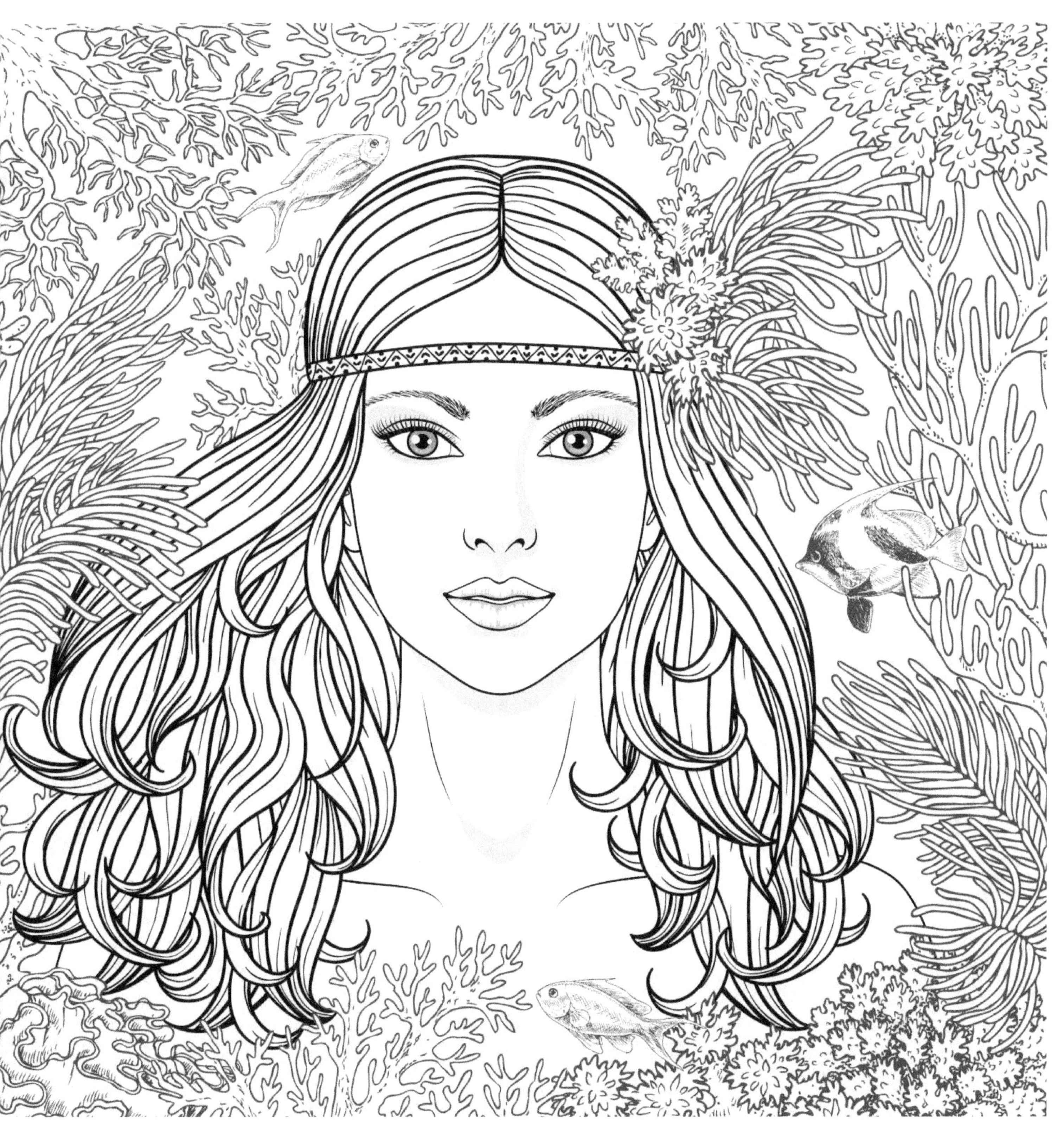

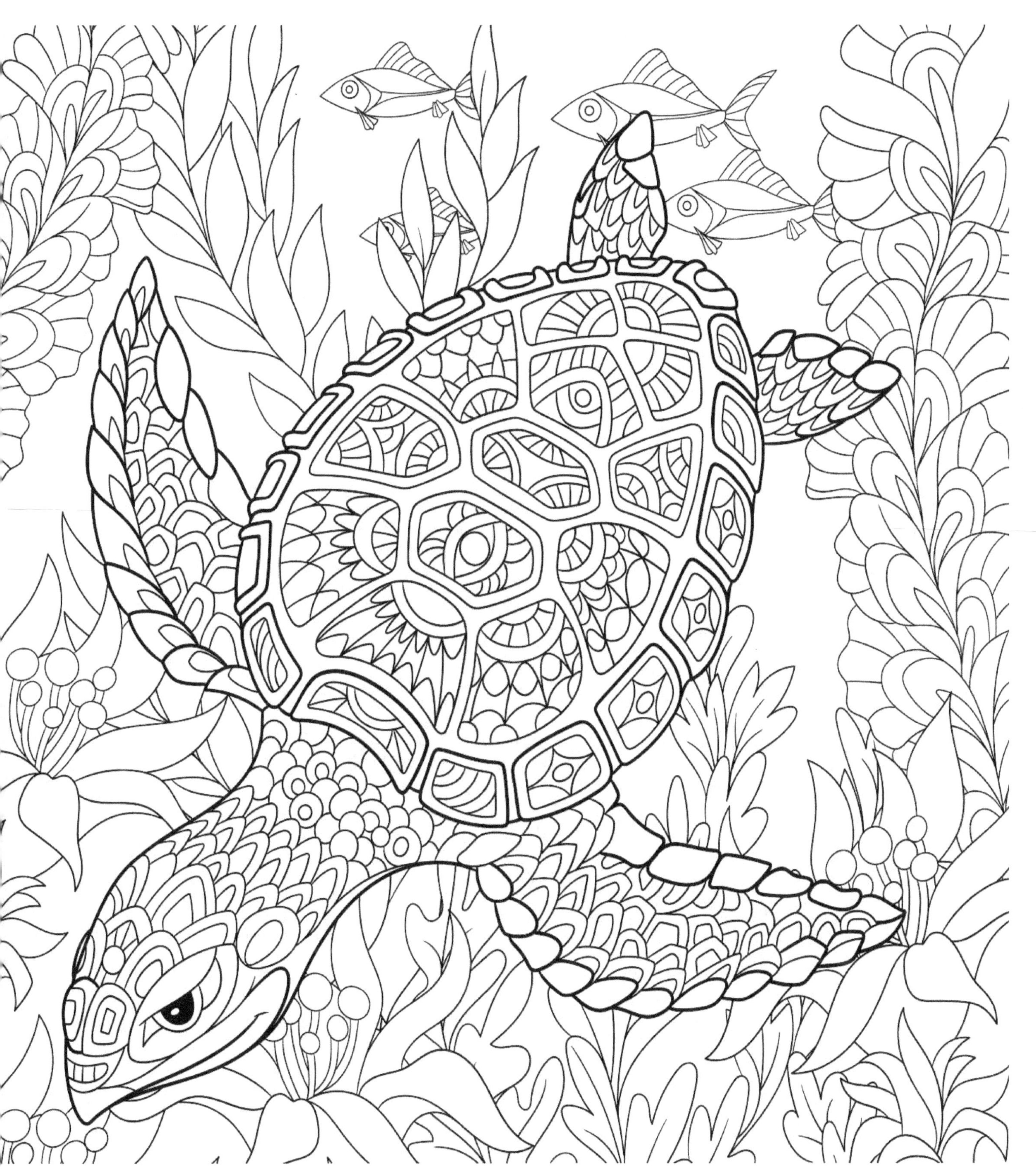

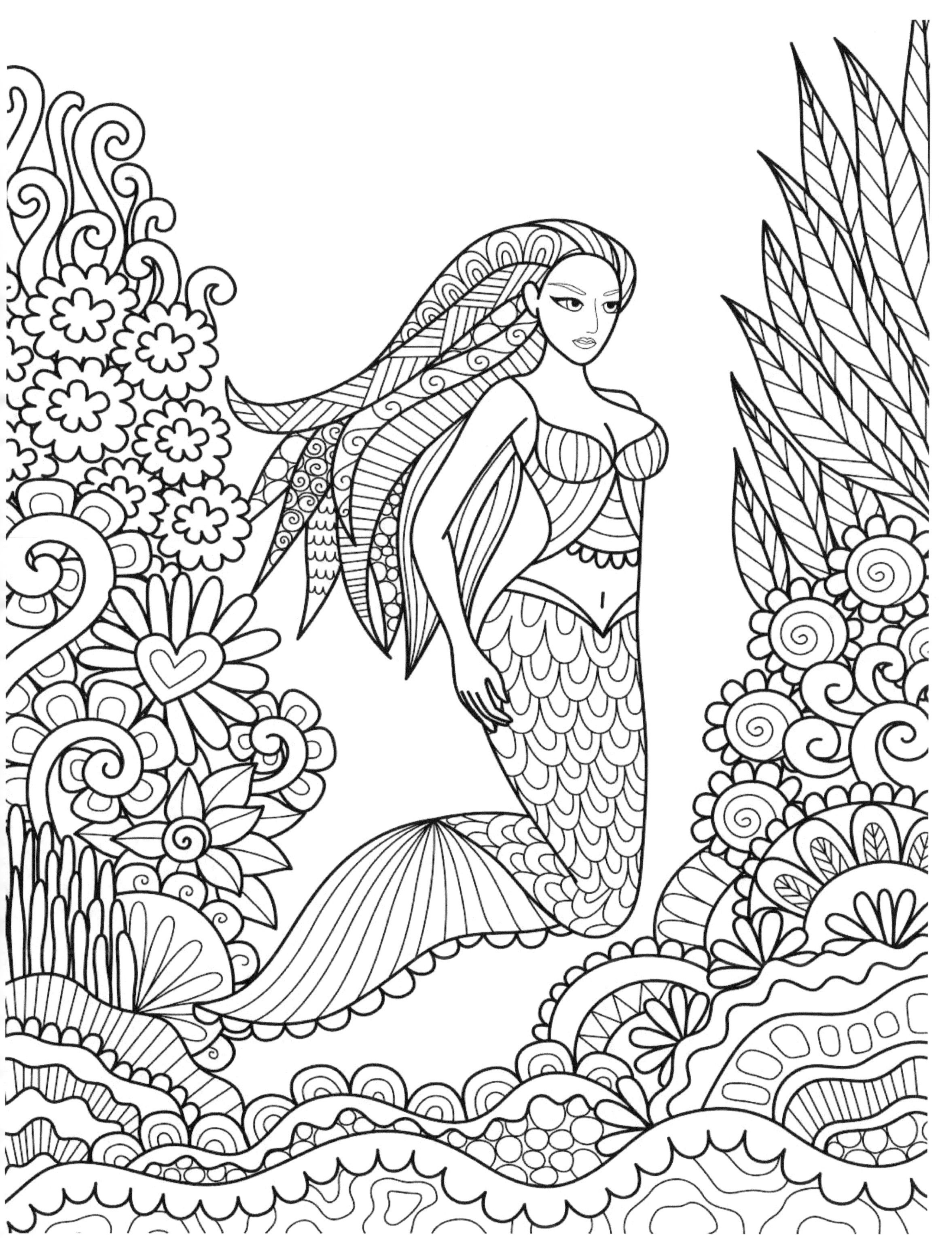

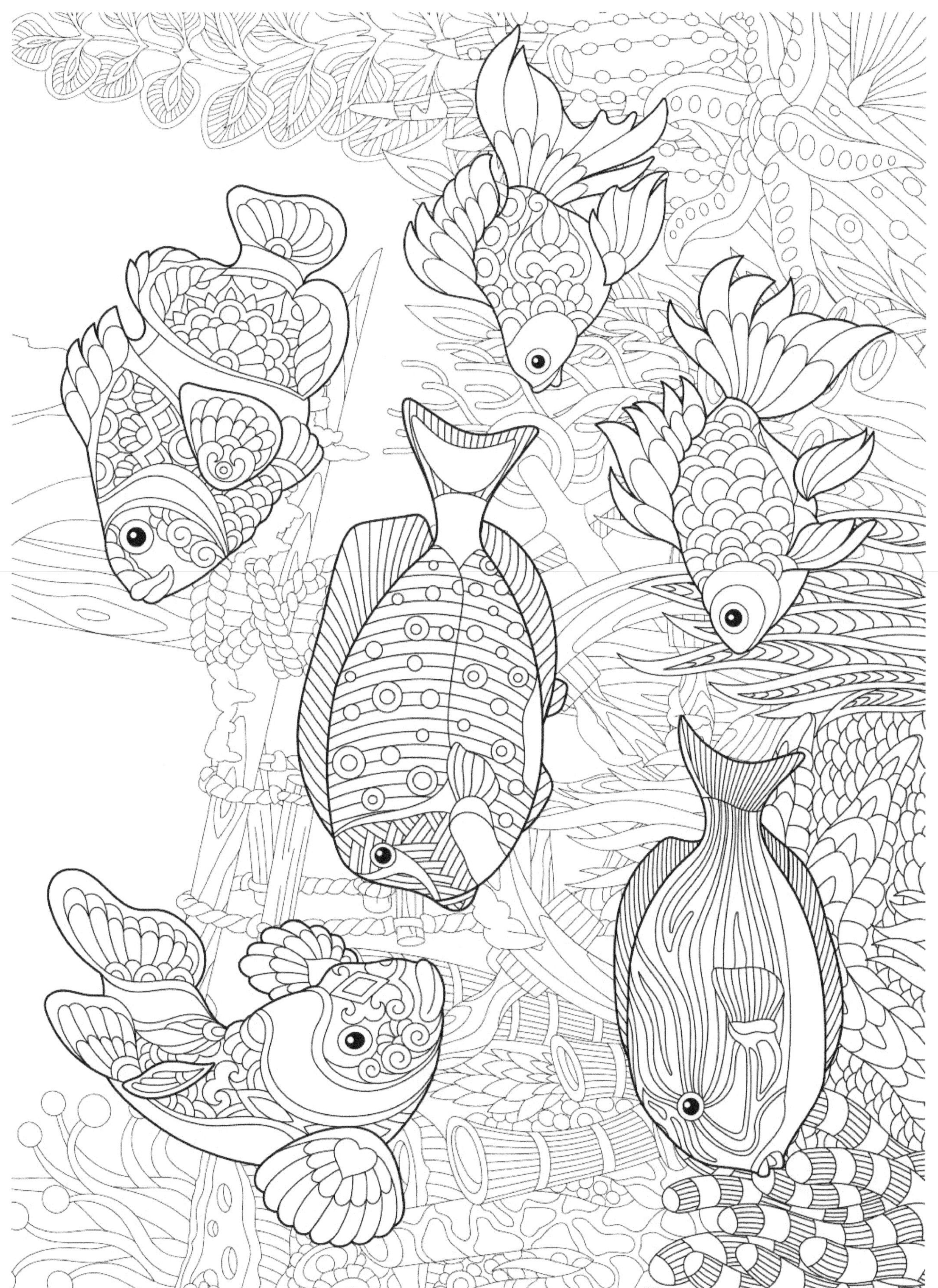

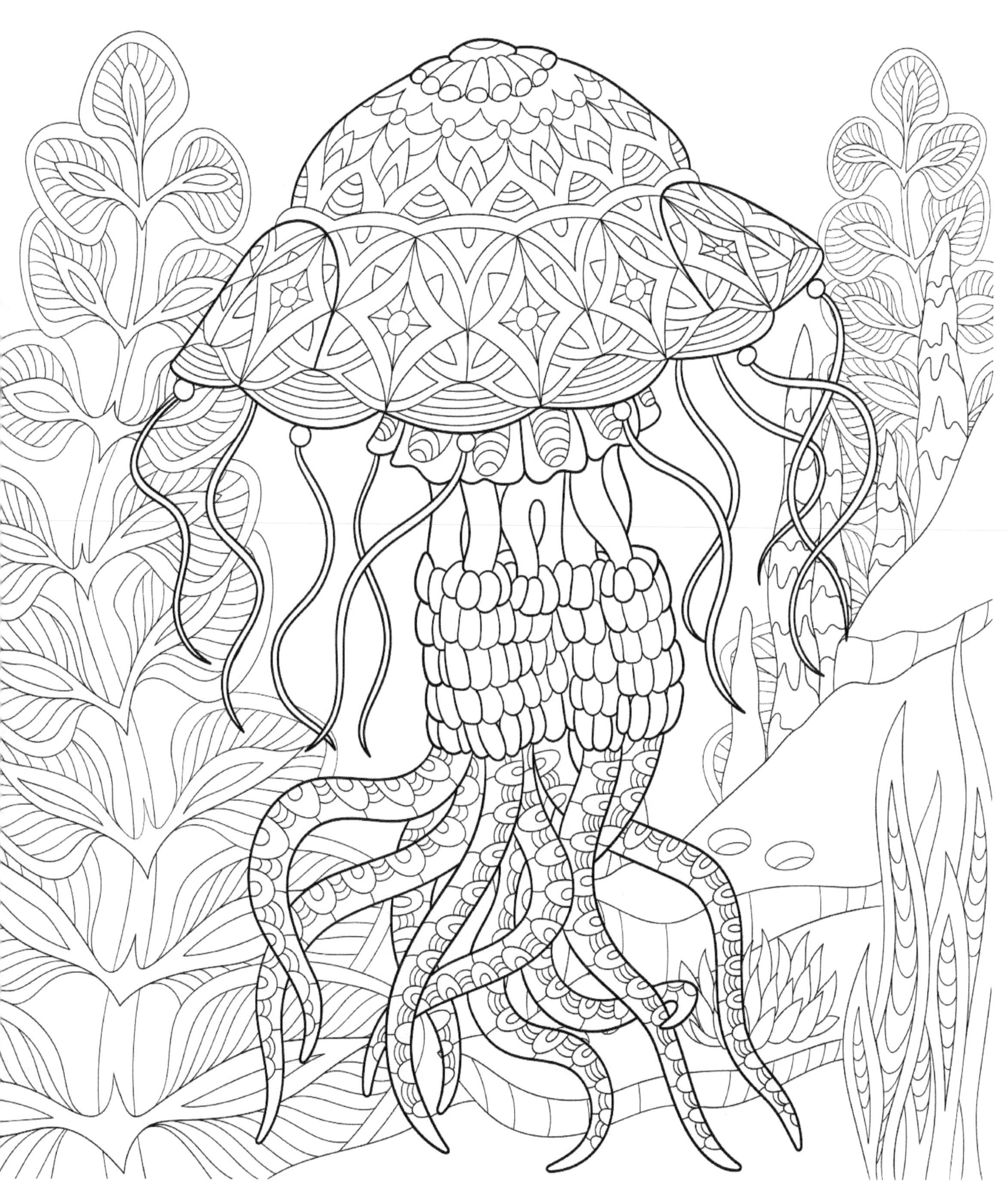

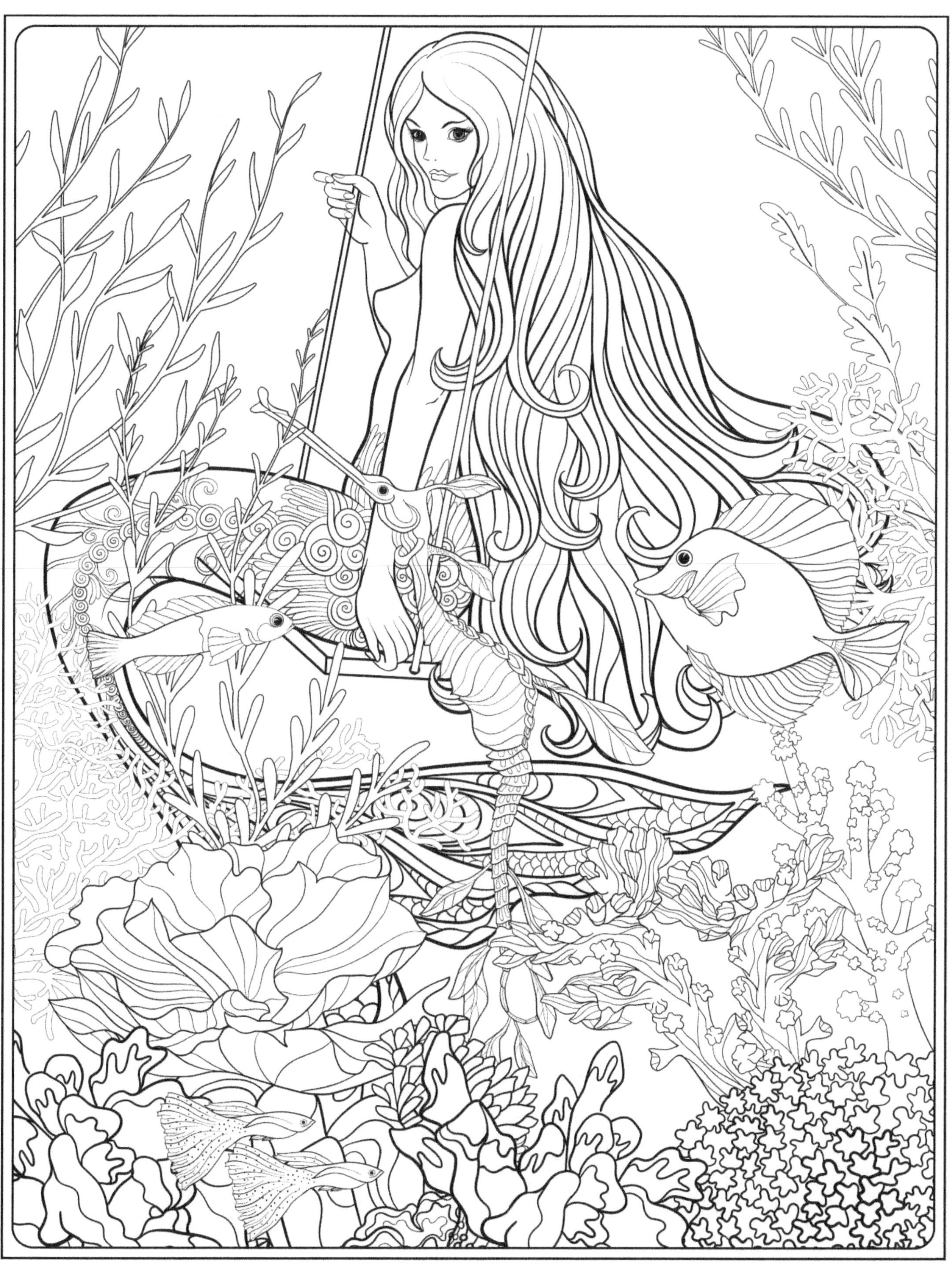

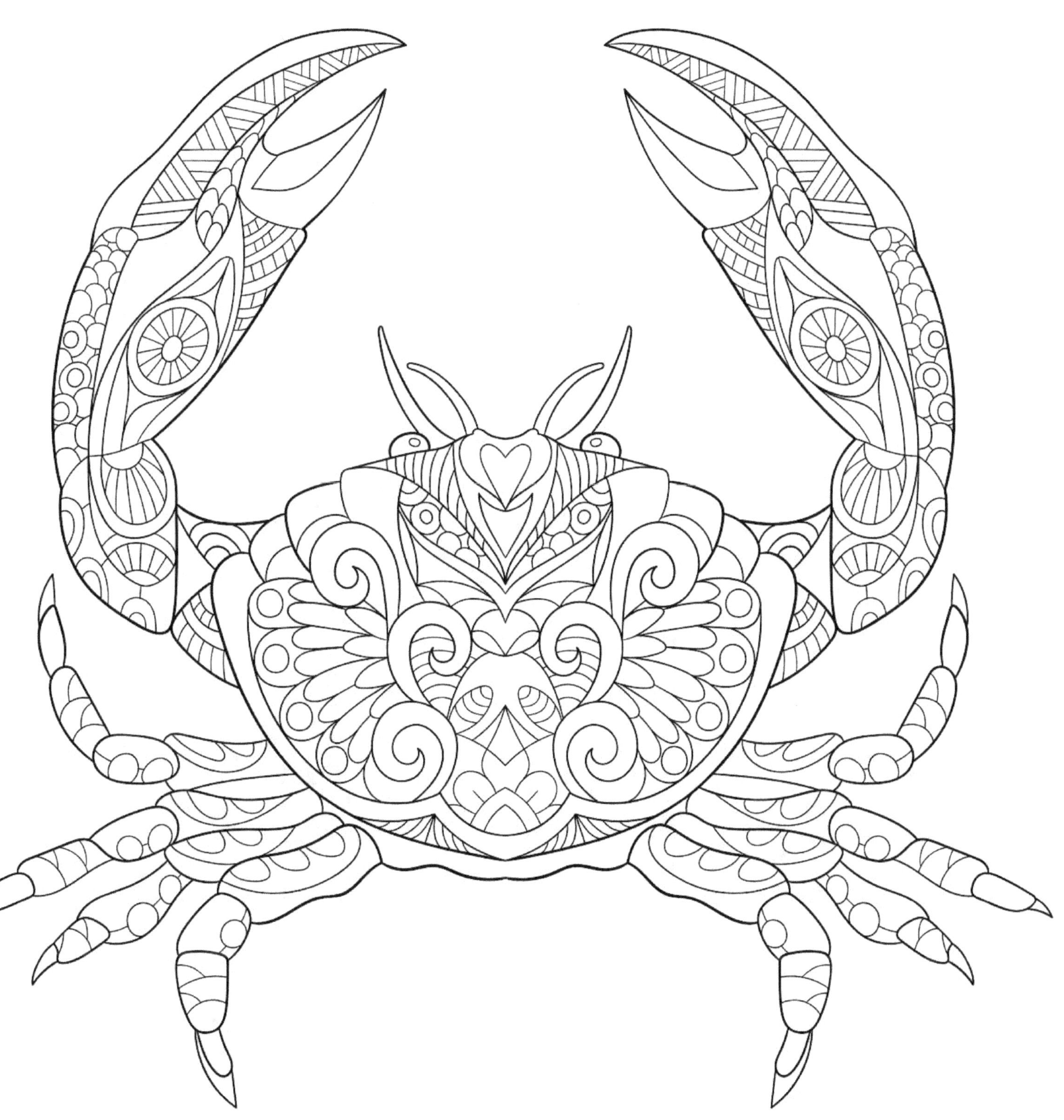

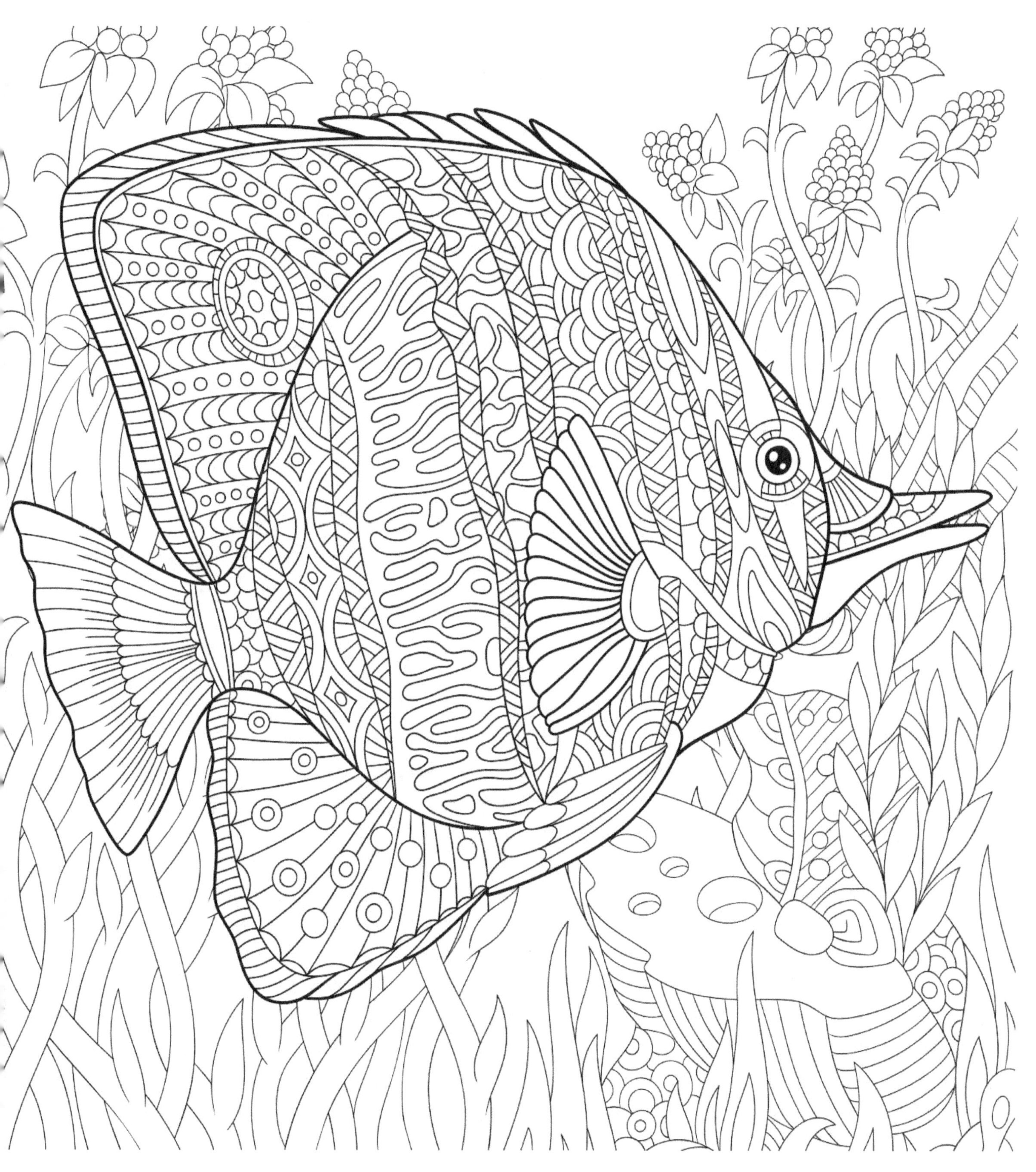

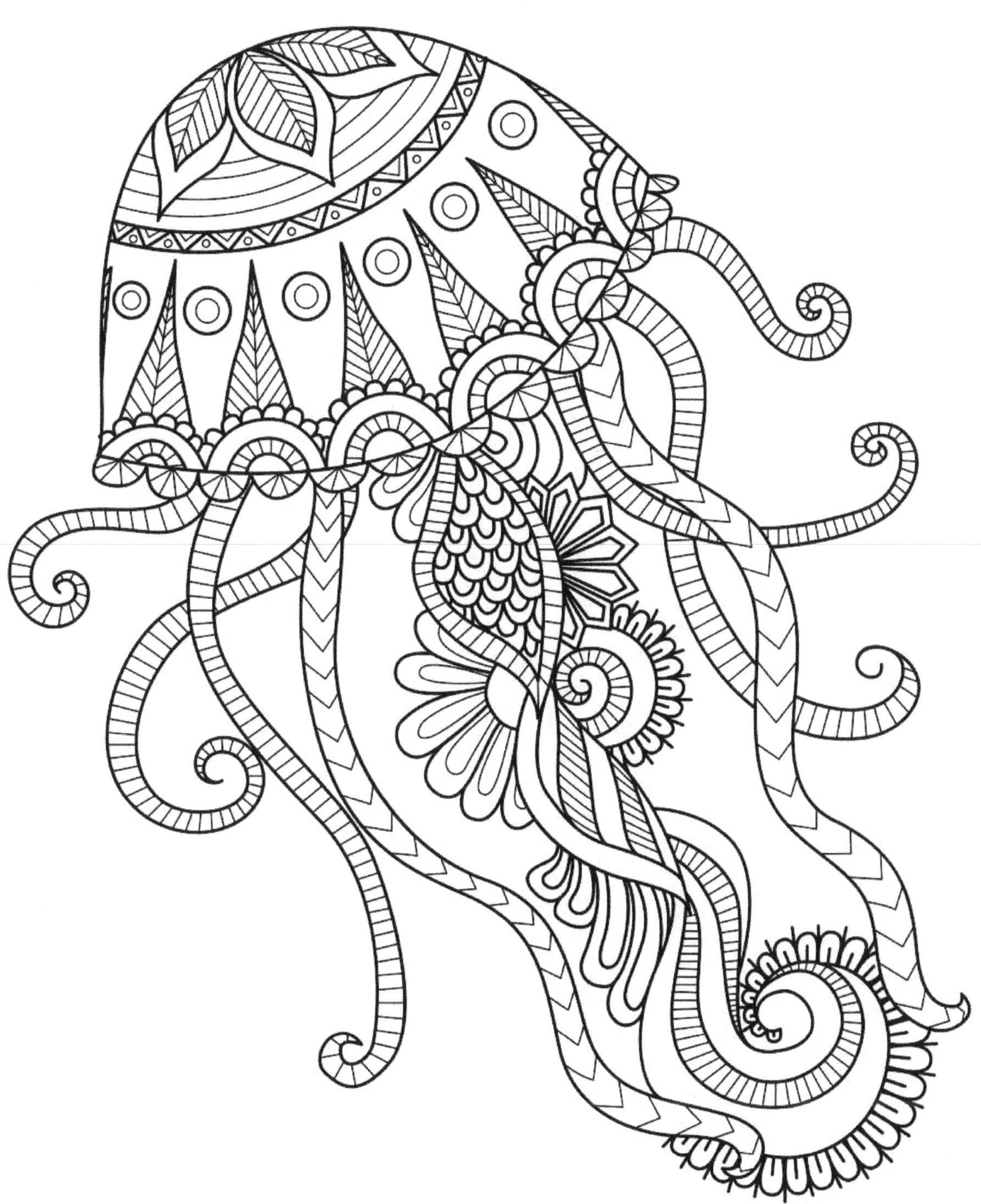

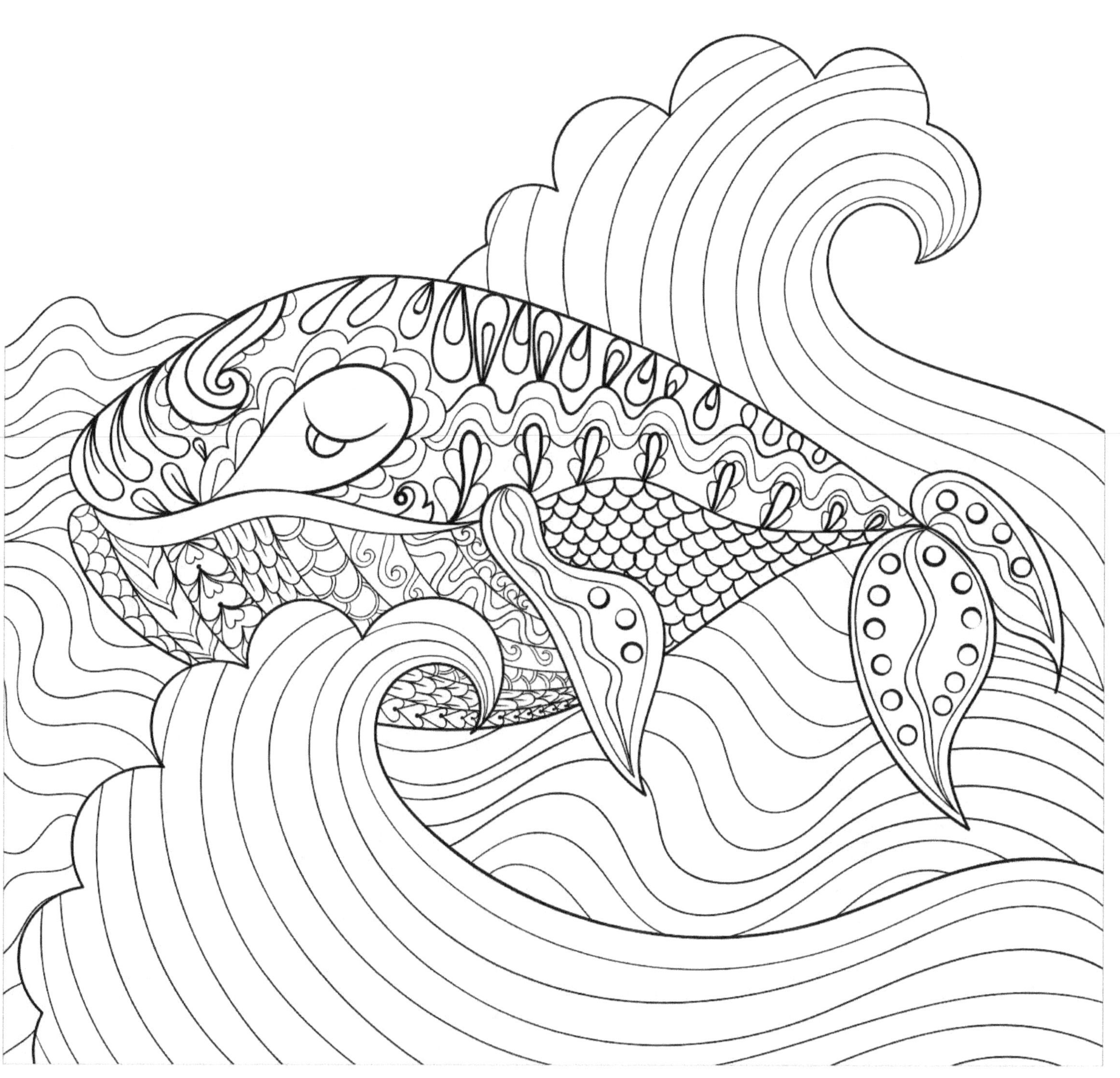

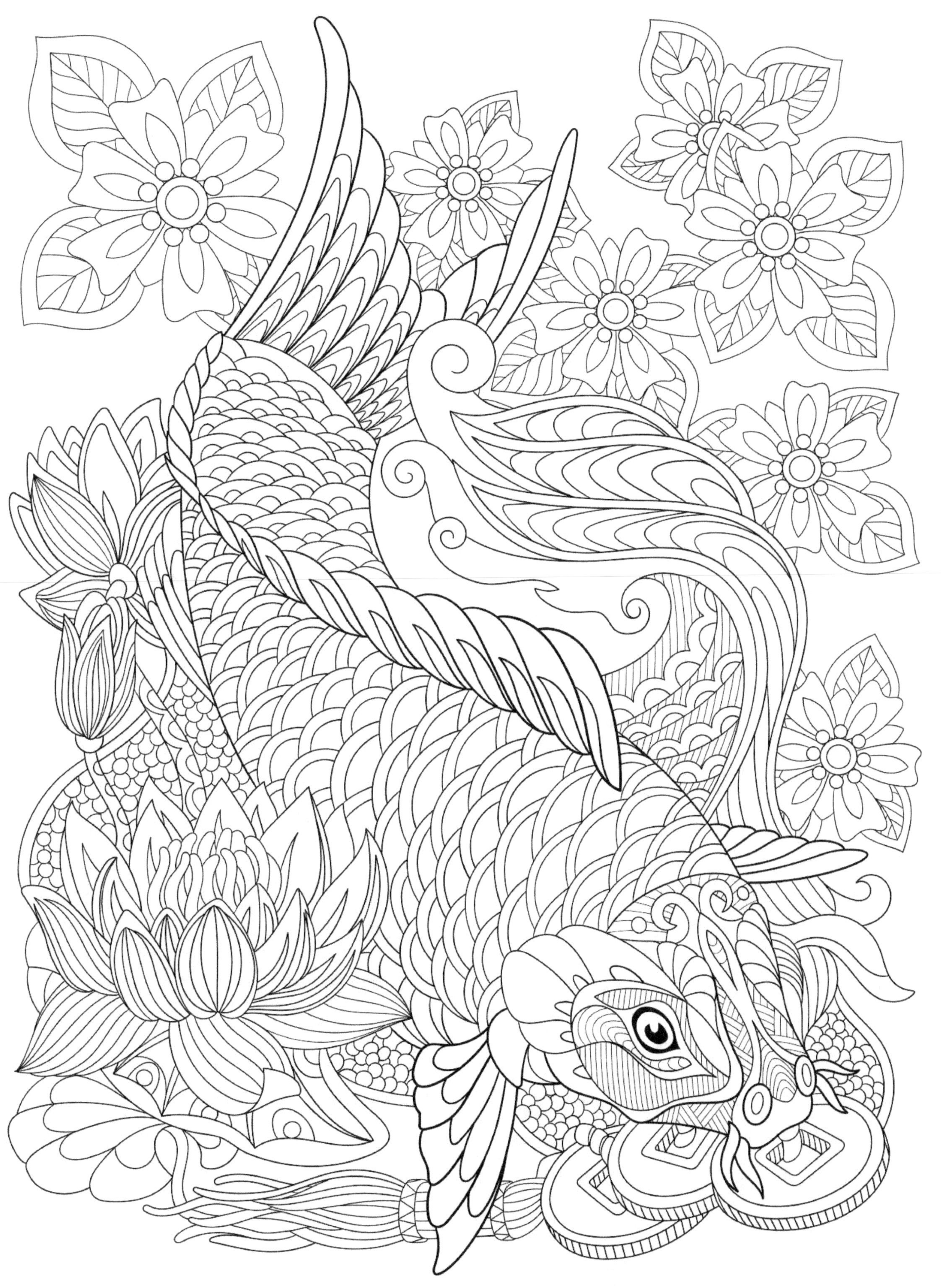

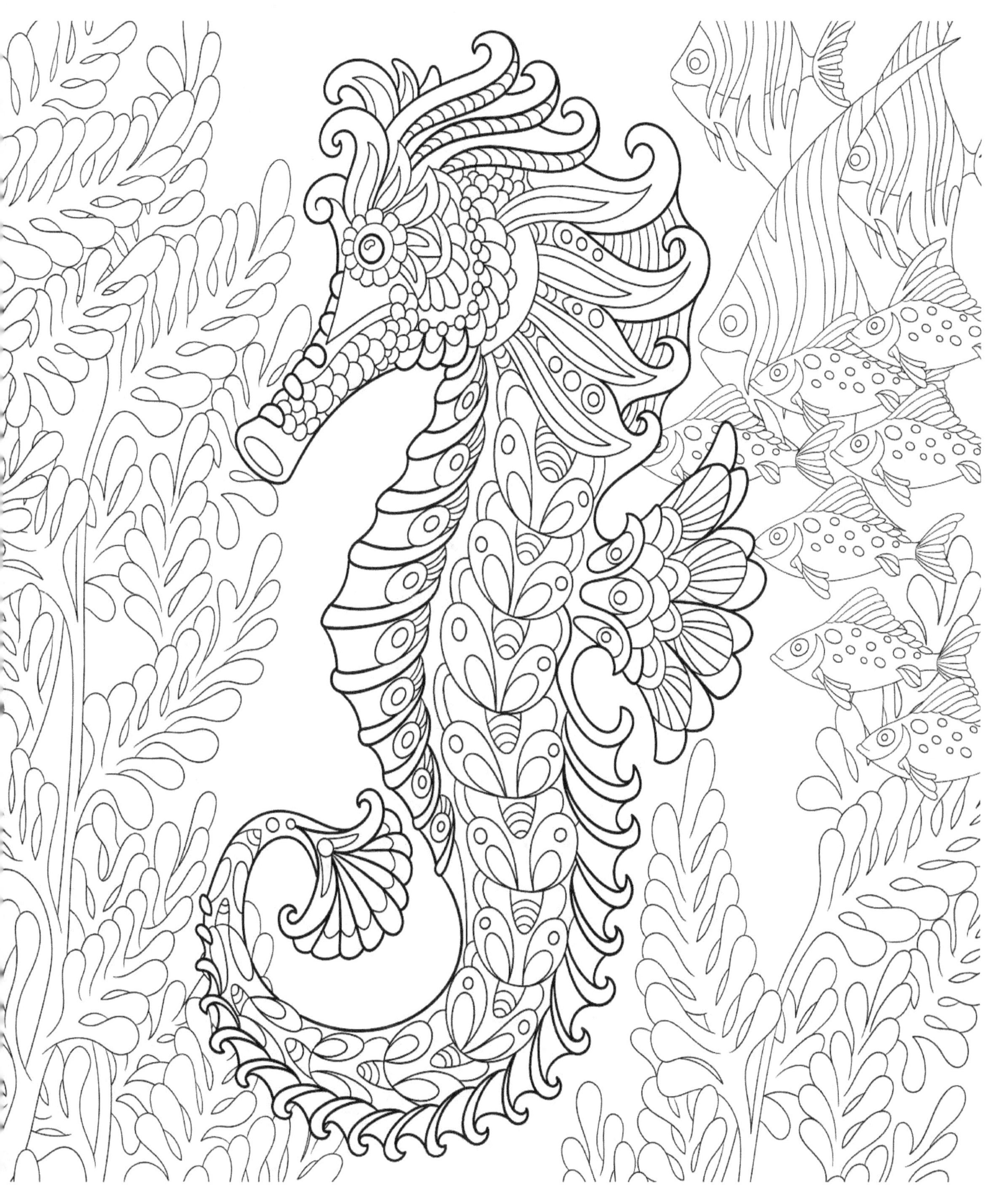

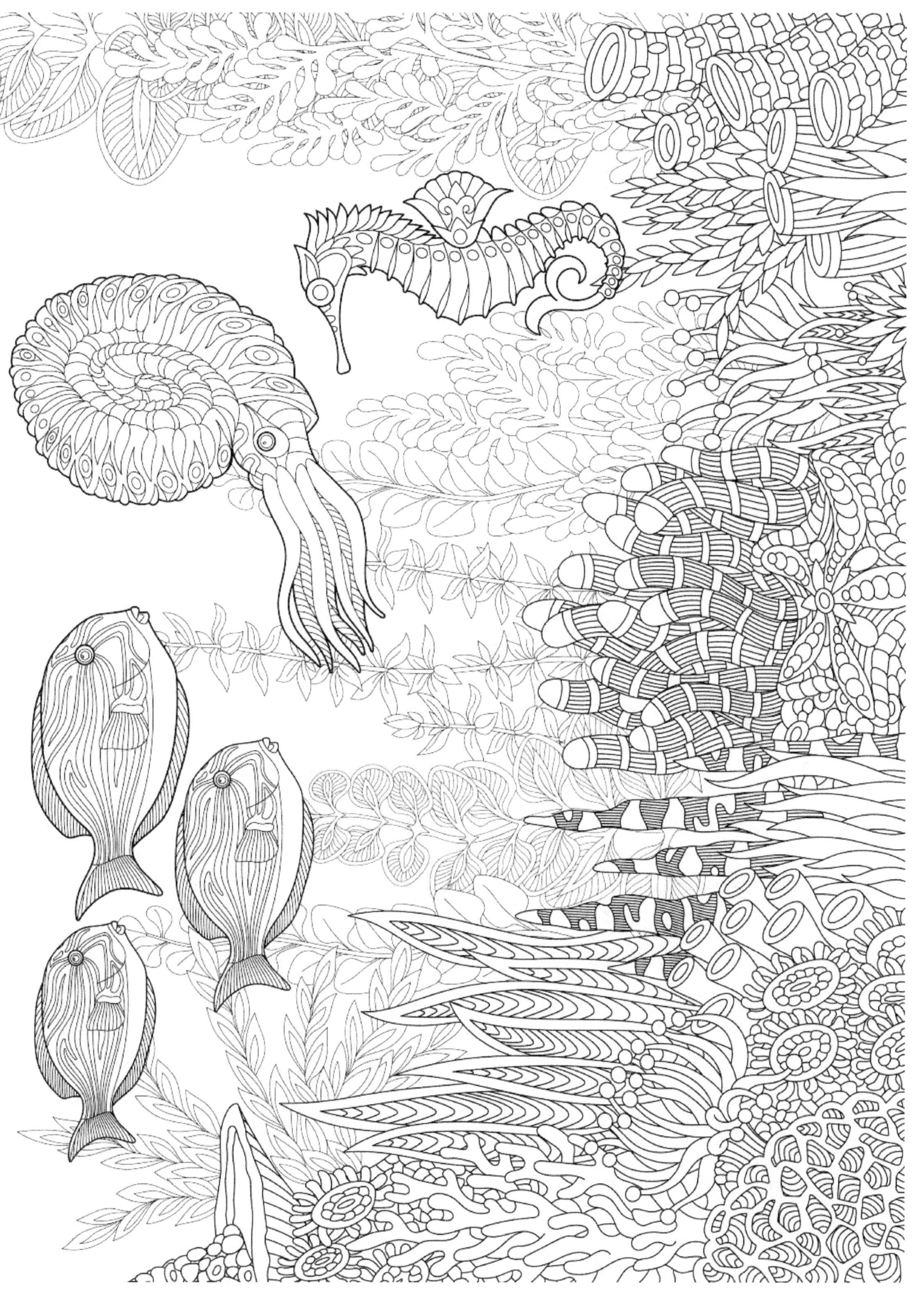

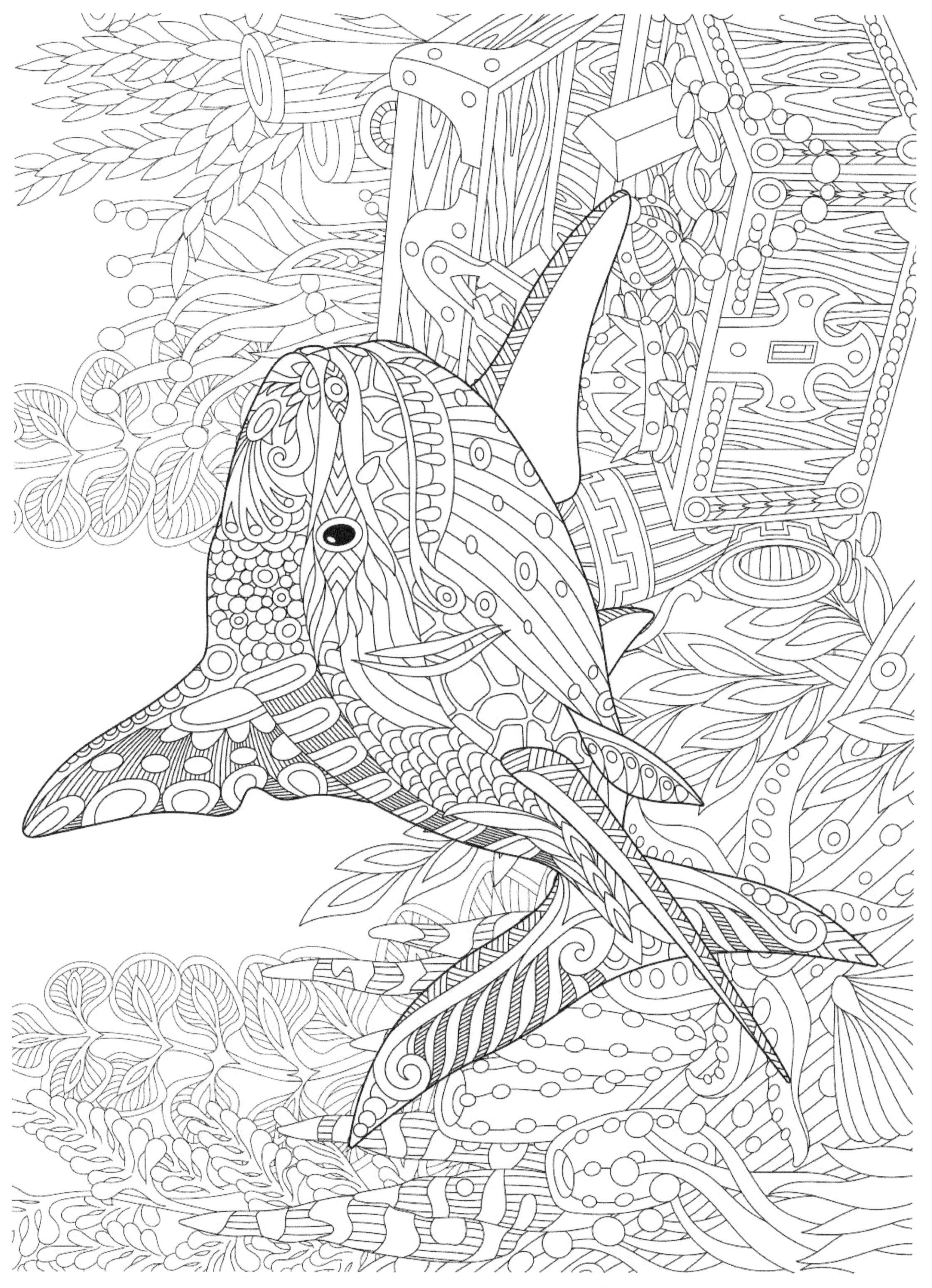

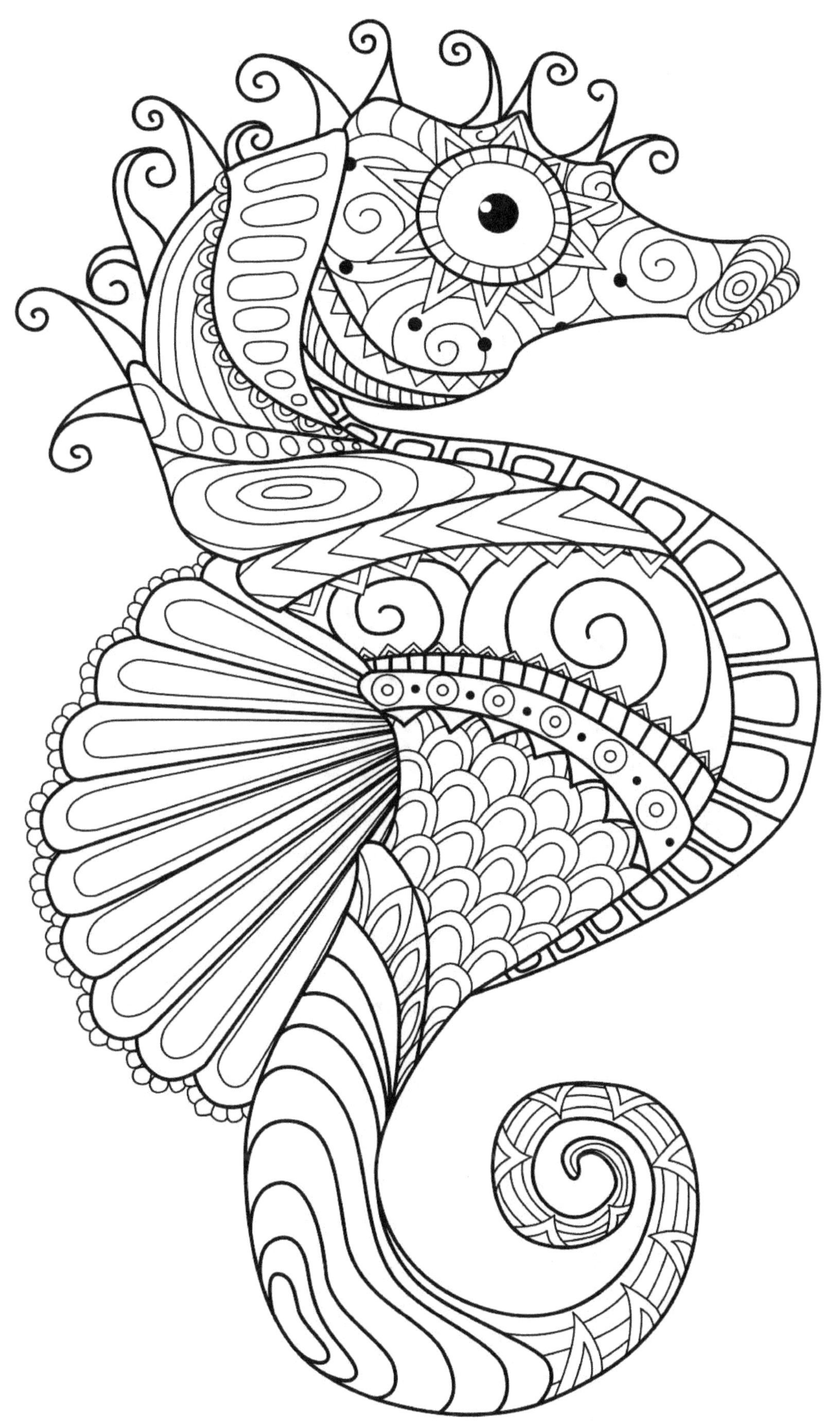

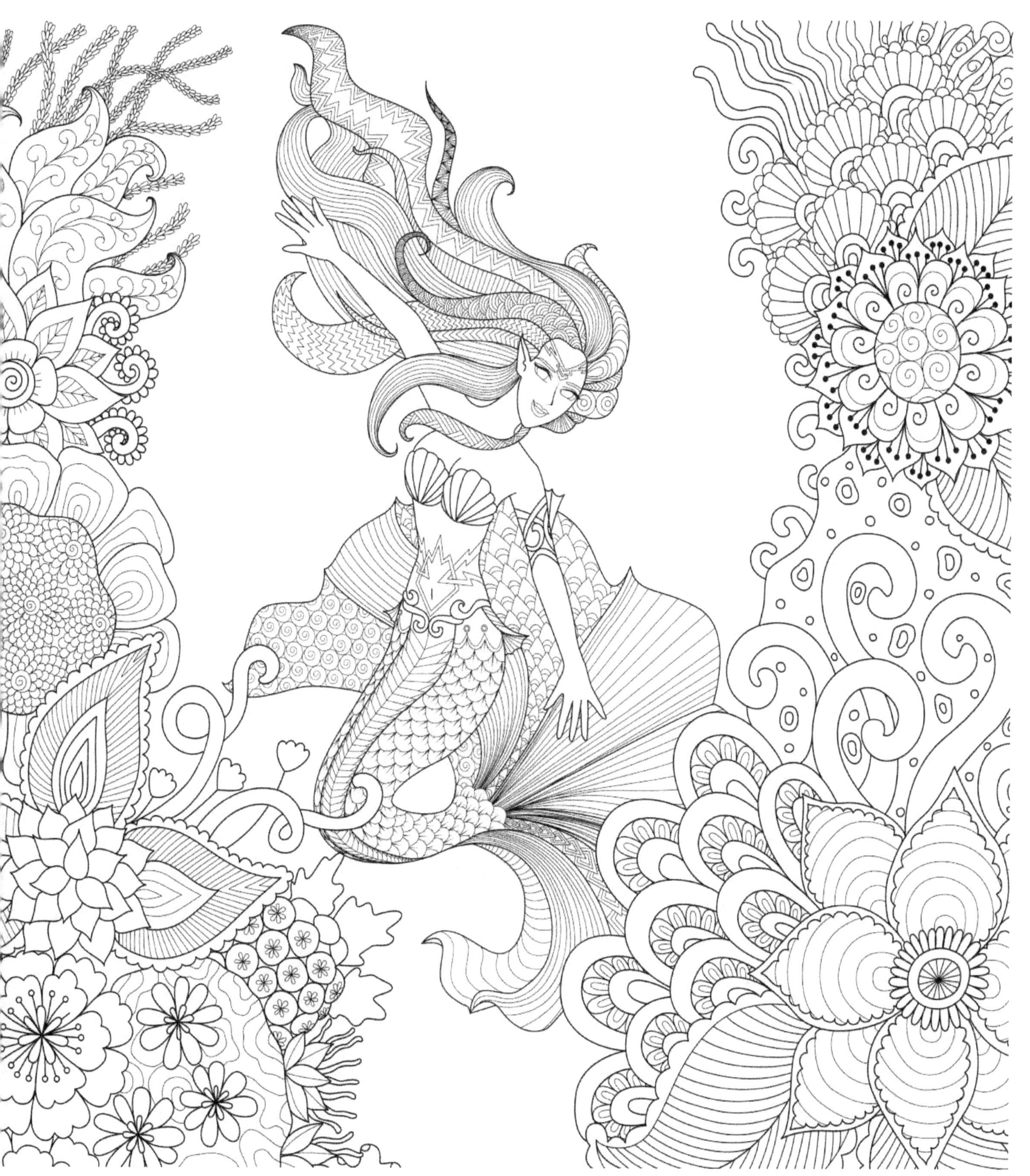

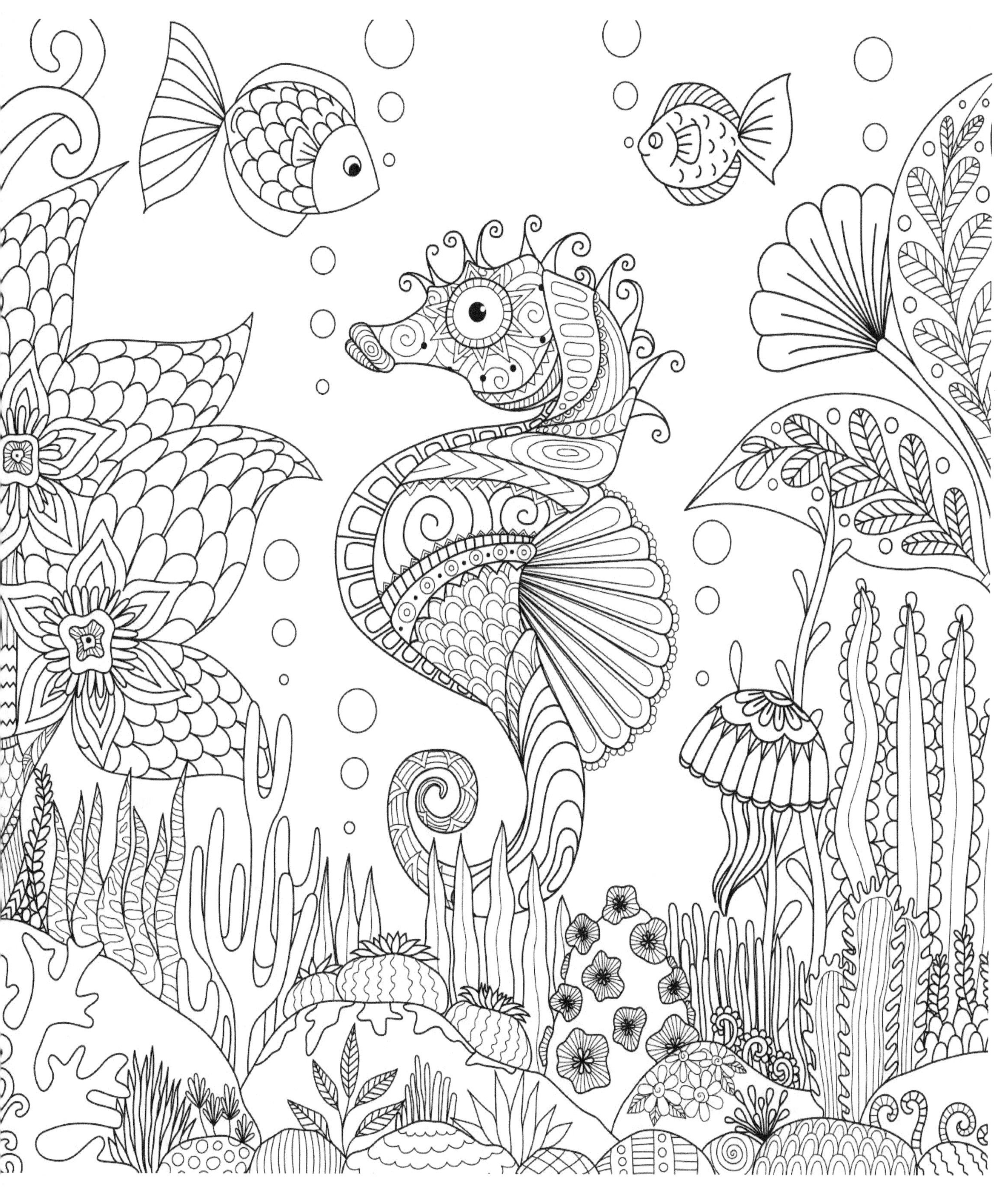

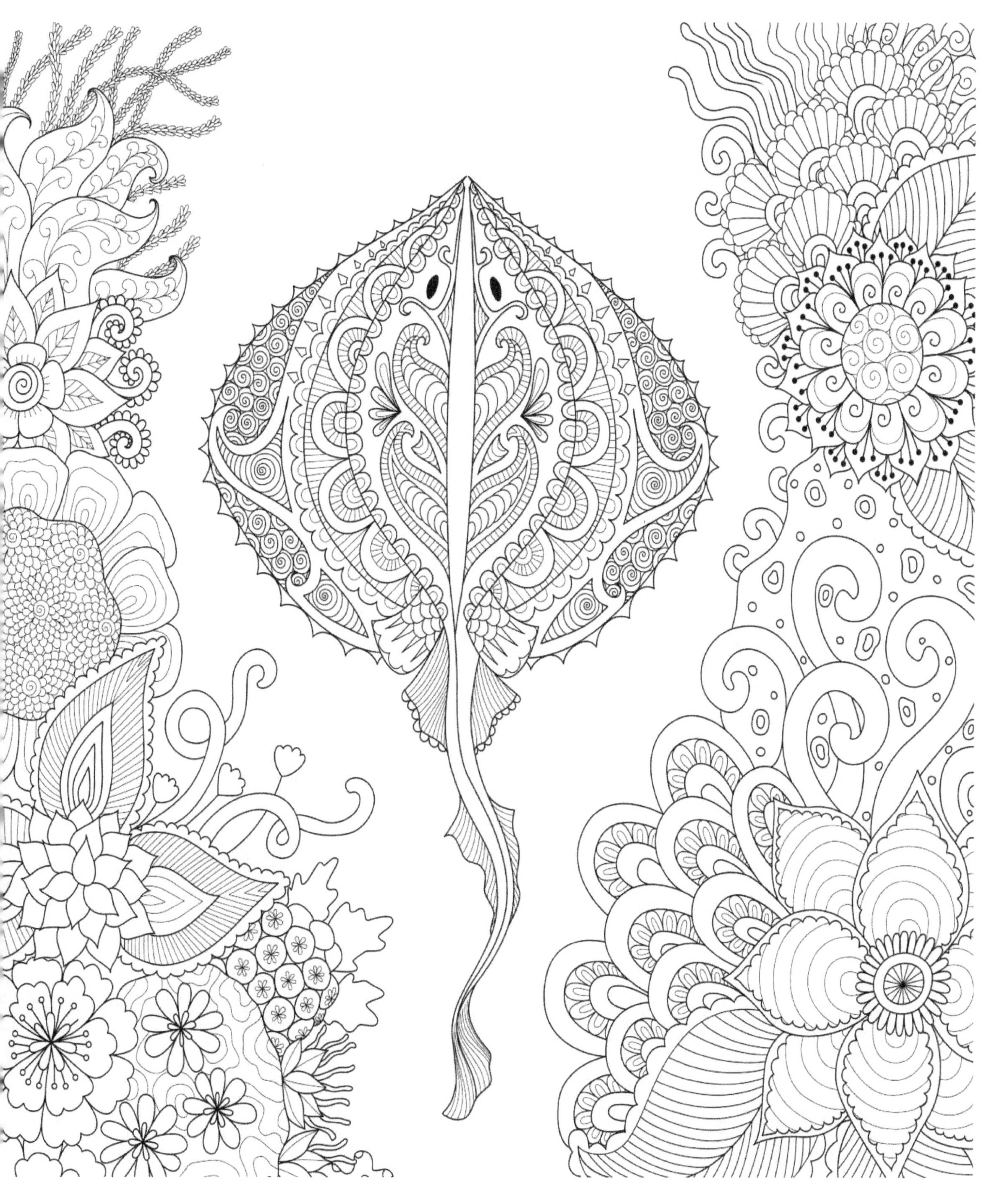

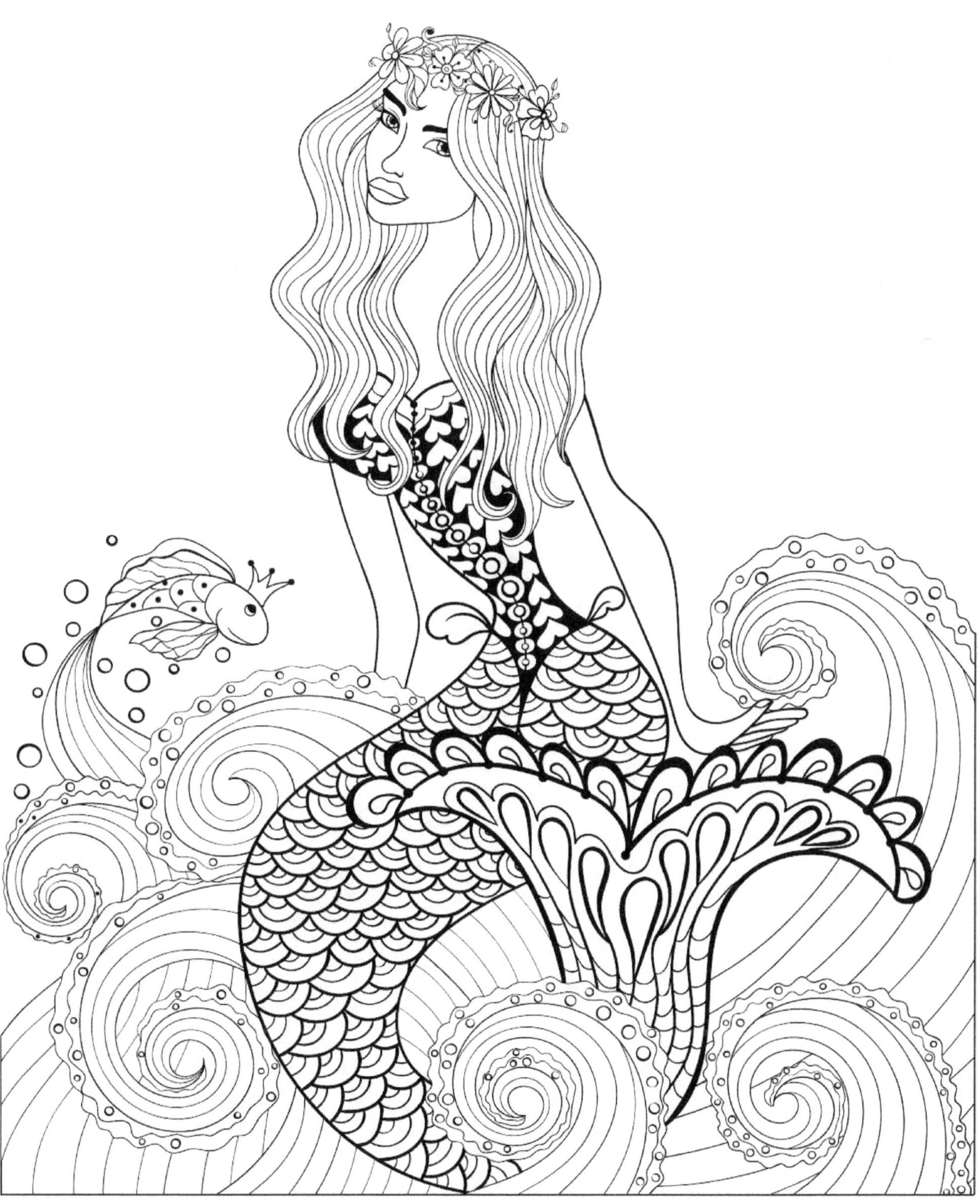

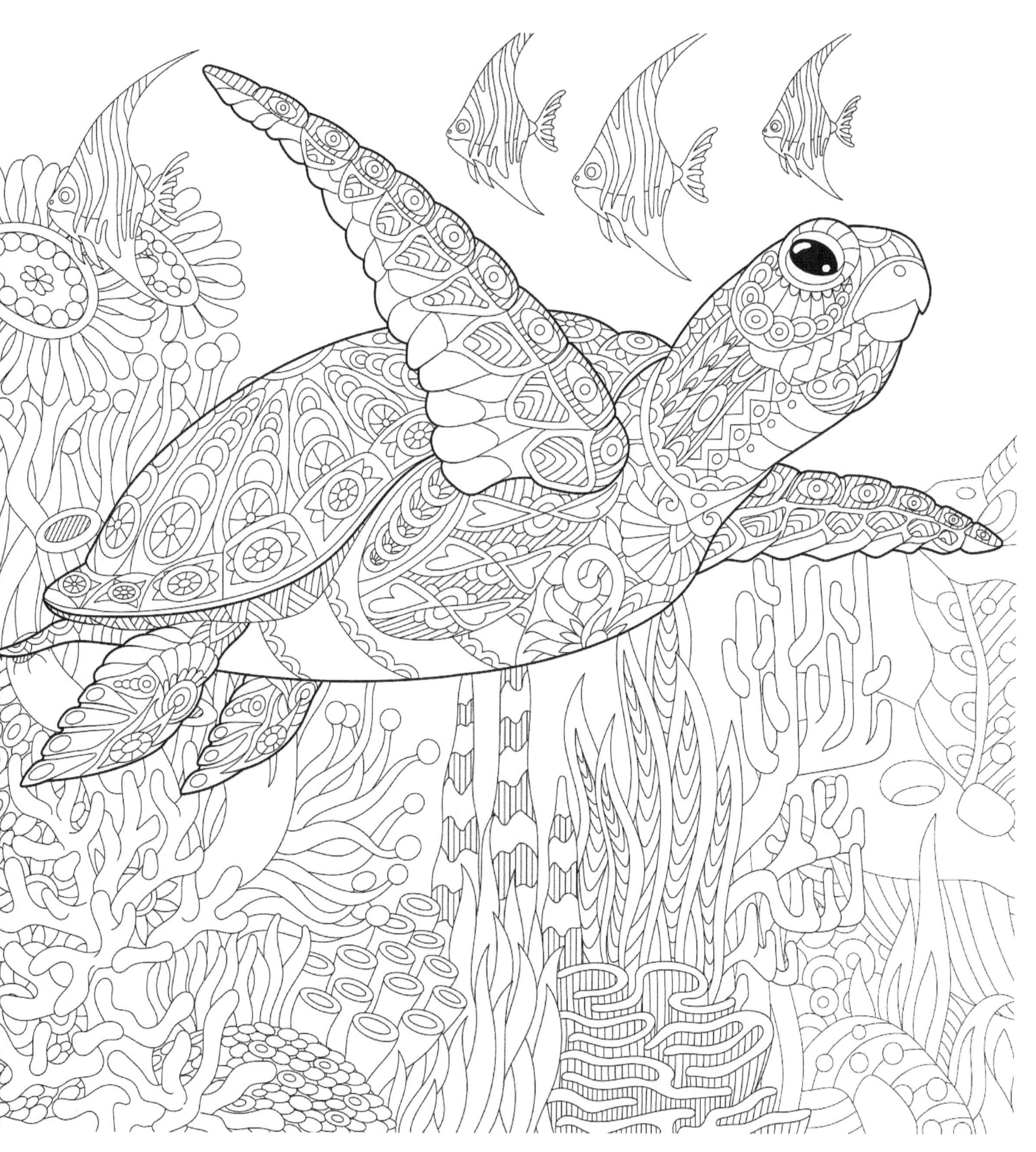

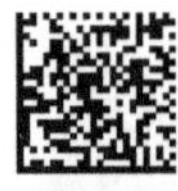

www.ingramcontent.com/pod-product-compliance
Lightning Source LLC
Chambersburg PA
CBHW080815280726
48660CB00018B/3450